Author's

This book features 100 influential and inspiring quotes by Mark Twain. Undoubtedly, this collection will give you a huge boost of inspiration.

1

"If you tell the truth, you don't have to remember anything."

2

"Good friends, good books, and a sleepy conscience: this is the ideal life."

3

"Whenever you find yourself on the side of the majority, it is time to reform (or pause and reflect)."

4

"The man who does not read has no advantage over the man who cannot read."

5

"Never put off till tomorrow what may be done day after tomorrow just as well."

6

"'Classic' – a book which people praise and don't read."

7

"I have never let my schooling interfere with my education."

8

"The fear of death follows from the fear of life. A man who lives fully is prepared to die at any time."

9

"A lie can travel half way around the world while the truth is putting on its shoes."

10

"Never tell the truth to people
who are not worthy of it."

11

"Keep away from people who try to belittle your ambitions. Small people always do that, but the really great make you feel that you, too, can become great."

12

"In a good bookroom you feel in some mysterious way that you are absorbing the wisdom contained in all the books through your skin, without even opening them."

13

"Substitute 'damn' every time you're inclined to write 'very;' your editor will delete it and the writing will be just as it should be."

14

"Reader, suppose you were an idiot. And suppose you were a member of Congress. But I repeat myself."

15

"Don't go around saying the world owes you a living. The world owes you nothing. It was here first."

16

"I did not attend his funeral, but
I sent a nice letter saying I
approved of it."

17

"God created war so that Americans would learn geography."

18

"I was gratified to be able to answer promptly, and I did. I said I didn't know."

19

"Never allow someone to be your priority while allowing yourself to be their option."

20

"But who prays for Satan? Who, in eighteen centuries, has had the common humanity to pray for the one sinner that needed it most?"

21

"The difference between the almost right word and the right word is really a large matter. 'tis the difference between the lightning bug and the lightning."

22

"Loyalty to country ALWAYS. Loyalty to government, when it deserves it."

23

"Truth is stranger than fiction, but it is because Fiction is obliged to stick to possibilities; Truth isn't."

24

"I do not fear death. I had been dead for billions and billions of years before I was born, and had not suffered the slightest inconvenience from it."

25

"Wrinkles should merely indicate where the smiles have been."

26

"Books are for people who wish they were somewhere else."

27

"What would men be without women? Scarce, sir...mighty scarce."

28

"Sanity and happiness are an impossible combination."

29

"When I was a boy of 14, my father was so ignorant I could hardly stand to have the old man around. But when I got to be 21, I was astonished at how much the old man had learned in seven years."

30

"Don't part with your illusions. When they are gone you may still exist, but you have ceased to live."

31

"Travel is fatal to prejudice, bigotry, and narrow-mindedness, and many of our people need it sorely on these accounts. Broad, wholesome, charitable views of men and things cannot be acquired by vegetating in one little corner of the earth all one's lifetime."

32

"Clothes make the man. Naked people have little or no influence on society."

33

"You can't depend on your eyes when your imagination is out of focus."

34

"Everyone is a moon, and has a
dark side which he never shows
to anybody."

35

"If you pick up a starving dog and make him prosperous he will not bite you. This is the principal difference between a dog and man."

36

"If you don't read the
newspaper, you're uninformed.
If you read the newspaper,
you're mis-informed."

37

"Always do what is right. It will gratify half of mankind and astound the other."

38

"Courage is resistance to fear, mastery of fear - not absence of fear."

"The trouble is not in dying for a friend, but in finding a friend worth dying for."

40

"Kindness is a language which the deaf can hear and the blind can see."

41

"It's not the size of the dog in the fight, it's the size of the fight in the dog."

42

"I've lived through some terrible things in my life, some of which actually happened."

43

"Education: the path from cocky ignorance to miserable uncertainty."

"The best way to cheer yourself is to try to cheer someone else up."

45

"Name the greatest of all inventors. Accident."

46

"You believe in a book that has talking animals, wizards, witches, demons, sticks turning into snakes, burning bushes, food falling from the sky, people walking on water, and all sorts of magical, absurd and primitive stories, and you say that we are the ones that need help?"

47

"The easy confidence with which I know another man's religion is folly teaches me to suspect that my own is also."

48

"The worst loneliness is to not be comfortable with yourself."

49

"All you need in this life is ignorance and confidence; then success is sure."

50

"The secret to getting ahead is getting started."

51

"History doesn't repeat itself,
but it does rhyme."

52

"A clear conscience is the sure
sign of a bad memory."

53

"Get your facts first, and then you can distort them as much as you please."

54

"If animals could speak, the dog would be a blundering outspoken fellow; but the cat would have the rare grace of never saying a word too much."

55

"If animals could speak, the dog would be a blundering outspoken fellow; but the cat would have the rare grace of never saying a word too much."

56

"I haven't any right to criticize books, and I don't do it except when I hate them. I often want to criticize Jane Austen, but her books madden me so that I can't conceal my frenzy from the reader; and therefore I have to stop every time I begin. Every time I read Pride and Prejudice I want to dig her up and beat her over the skull with her own shin-bone."

57

"Forgiveness is the fragrance that the violet sheds on the heel that has crushed it."

58

"A banker is a fellow who lends you his umbrella when the sun is shining, but wants it back the minute it begins to rain."

59

"Out of all the things I have lost,
I miss my mind the most."

60

"I didn't have time to write a short letter, so I wrote a long one instead."

61

"April 1. This is the day upon which we are reminded of what we are on the other three hundred and sixty-four."

62

"Never argue with stupid
people, they will drag you down
to their level and then beat you
with experience."

63

"I have found out that there ain't no surer way to find out whether you like people or hate them than to travel with them."

64

"To get the full value of joy you must have someone to divide it with."

65

"When angry, count four. When very angry, swear."

66

"Of all the animals, man is the only one that is cruel. He is the only one that inflicts pain for the pleasure of doing it."

67

"Any emotion, if it is sincere, is involuntary."

68

"Heaven goes by favor. If it went by merit, you would stay out and your dog would go in."

69

"I must have a prodigious amount of mind; it takes me as much as a week, sometimes, to make it up!"

70

"It is curious that physical courage should be so common in the world and moral courage so rare."

71

"The most interesting information come from children, for they tell all they know and then stop."

72

"After all these years, I see that I was mistaken about Eve in the beginning; it is better to live outside the Garden with her than inside it without her."

73

"Anger is an acid that can do more harm to the vessel in which it is stored than to anything on which it is poured."

74

"When we remember we are all mad, the mysteries disappear and life stands explained."

75

"The human race has only one really effective weapon and that is laughter."

76

"Adam was but human—this explains it all. He did not want the apple for the apple's sake, he wanted it only because it was forbidden. The mistake was in not forbidding the serpent; then he would have eaten the serpent."

77

"The Bible has noble poetry in it... and some good morals and a wealth of obscenity, and upwards of a thousand lies."

78

"The dog is a gentleman; I hope to go to his heaven not man's."

79

"Always acknowledge a fault. This will throw those in authority off their guard and give you an opportunity to commit more."

80

"Giving up smoking is the easiest thing in the world. I know because I've done it thousands of times."

81

"If voting made any difference they wouldn't let us do it."

82

"There is a charm about the forbidden that makes it unspeakably desirable."

83

"I've had a lot of worries in my life, most of which never happened."

84

"Eat a live frog first thing in the morning and nothing worse will happen to you the rest of the day."

85

"Of all God's creatures, there is only one that cannot be made slave of the leash. That one is the cat. If man could be crossed with the cat it would improve the man, but it would deteriorate the cat."

86

"Reality can be beaten with enough imagination."

87

"I have a higher and grander standard of principle than George Washington. He could not lie; I can, but I won't."

88

"There are many humorous things in the world; among them, the white man's notion that he is less savage than the other savages."

89

"Education consists mainly of
what we have unlearned."

90

"Part of the secret of success in life is to eat what you like and let the food fight it out inside."

"It is better to deserve honors and not have them than to have them and not deserve them."

"Action speaks louder than words but not nearly as often."

93

"My books are water; those of the great geniuses is wine. Everybody drinks water."

"It's better to keep your mouth shut and appear stupid than open it and remove all doubt"

95

"There was never yet an uninteresting life. Such a thing is an impossibility. Inside of the dullest exterior there is a drama, a comedy, and a tragedy."

"It takes your enemy and your friend, working together, to hurt you to the heart: the one to slander you and the other to get the news to you."

97

"It's easier to fool people than to convince them that they have been fooled."

98

"In the beginning of a change the patriot is a scarce man, and brave, and hated and scorned. When his cause succeeds, the timid join him, for then it costs nothing to be a patriot."

"The right word may be effective, but no word was ever as effective as a rightly timed pause."

100

"If Christ were here there is one thing he would not be—a Christian."

Printed in Great Britain
by Amazon

83393815R10058